Between Heaven and Earth

Between Heaven and Earth

Poems, Prayers, Pictures

Isobel de Gruchy

Foreword by Desmond Tutu

RESOURCE *Publications* • Eugene, Oregon

BETWEEN HEAVEN AND EARTH
Poems, Prayers, Pictures

Copyright © 2015 Isobel de Gruchy. All rights reserved. Except for brief quotations in critical publications or reviews, no part of this book may be reproduced in any manner without prior written permission from the publisher. Write: Permissions, Wipf and Stock Publishers, 199 W. 8th Ave., Suite 3, Eugene, OR 97401.

Resource Publications
An Imprint of Wipf and Stock Publishers
199 W. 8th Ave., Suite 3
Eugene, OR 97401

www.wipfandstock.com

ISBN 13: 978-1-4982-2274-7

Manufactured in the U.S.A.   07/23/2015

to John
who has walked life's journey with me
and whose love and support have been invaluable

and to Jeanelle and Anton
who are always there for me

Contents

Foreword by Desmond Tutu | xi
Preface | xiii
Notes for the Non-South African Reader | xv
Acknowledgments | xvii

Between Heaven and Earth | 1

EARTH
Spring | 3
Autumn | 4
Approaching Storm | 5
Afternoon Walk in Winter | 6
All Rivers Flow to the Sea | 7
Last Light | 8
Grape Flowers | 8
May is the Month for Mushrooms | 9
Ten Thousand Diamonds | 10
Robin in the Rain | 11
Sometimes a poem is like a caterpillar | 11
Waterfall | 12
The Orange River Gorge | 13
The Rock Thrush | 14
Snake | 15
The Wasp and the Spider | 17
Rainy Morning at the River | 18
The Flap of a Butterfly's Wings | 19
The Olive Thrush | 20
I Walk Alone at Dawn | 21
Yellow Daisy | 21
After the Fire | 22
Well-Spring | 22

vii

SELF
Who am I? | 24
Living in Between | 25
I am | 26
In the Mirror | 28
The Past | 29
Go to the Ant . . . | 30
Like a Stalagmite | 31
Insomnia | 32
Fountain | 33
First Kiss | 34
Past and Future | 35
 Full Circle | 36
The Milestone Marked Seventy | 37
On Our Golden Wedding Anniversary | 38
The Monster | 39
My Prayer as a Person with Parkinson's Disease | 40

OTHERS
Communication | 42
You Came into My Life | 42
Acrophobia | 43
Friendship | 44
A Bunch of Flowers | 45
A Death and a Birth | 46
My Love for You | 48
Is it Love? | 49
Connections | 49
I Pray Shalom for You | 51
When Good Things End | 53
Life is Unfair | 54
A Word Lightly Spoken | 55
My Prayer as I Interact Daily with Others | 56
Saying the Truth | 59
Seeing Through a Mist | 60
Come Inside With Me | 61
Dream World | 62
Alfred Mxhalisa | 63

Struggle Tapestry | 64
Walk On, Walk On. | 65
Looking Right Through | 66
Endings | 67

FUN

Ode to a Frenetic Old Lady | 69
Confabulation | 69
Contrary Creatures | 70
Going Uphill | 70
Rain Storm | 71
Time | 71
Saturday at Gran's | 72
Taking a Hike | 73
The Second Try | 73
The Lecture | 74
Procrastination | 74
Whale-Watching | 75
To the Little Mouse | 76

GOD

Morning Praise | 78
God in a Point | 79
Tree in the Desert | 80
Abraham's Call | 81
Mystery and Meaning | 81
No-one Knows my Name | 82
Christmas Morning, 2009 | 83
In Remembrance of Her | 84
Good Friday on Mauritius—A Prayer | 85
Easter Morning, 2009 | 86
Easter Morning, a Year Later | 87
Sonnet to Silence | 87
Jacob's Ladder | 88
Jacob Wrestles with God | 89
Can you Hear Your Name? | 90
Confession | 91
The Trees of Life | 92
Lord God of Power and Wisdom and Love | 93

Prayer for the New Year | 94
Keeping the Silence | 95
We Do Not Know | 96
Was it Easy for You, Jesus? | 97
Made in God's Image | 98
Be Perfect | 99
We Need Easter, Lord | 100
For Rachel's Children | 101
Massacre, Nairobi, 21 Sept 2013 | 102

HEAVEN
All Shall be Well, after Death? | 104
Dawn will Come | 105
Is Death only slipping through the door? | 106
Easter Message, 2010 | 107
I'm OK, I'm Alright | 108
You will not be Overcome | 110
In Well and in Woe | 111
Lifted and Carried | 112
Seeing Heaven Open | 113
To Steve and his Spirit | 115
Prayer on the First Anniversary of Steve's Death | 116
Out of Death Comes Life | 117
I am the Ghost of Christmas Past | 119
The Curtain between two Worlds | 120
When I Think Olive | 121
The Chasm between Life and Death | 125
Heaven is Here Too | 126

Bibliography | 127

Foreword

We have here a great gift to us all. As we page through this anthology with its poems about sunsets, about spiders and snakes, about Parkinson's disease, about the shattering loss of a dearly loved one, we give thanks to God for that crisis in relationships that shook Isobel so much that she sought solace in writing poetry, self-taught out of a deep need. In saying this we are not callous or sadistic. No, we are honoring a great gift that might not have developed had that crisis not occurred.

This is a beautiful anthology describing nature beautifully, gently, as if we could, from the page, go and touch the wasp struggling with the burden it is pulling to its nest, witness the breaking of dawn, stand breathless as we watch with her the slithering snake that enters her house and having satisfied itself, slithers out again. Many of the nature poems are that but more, if we are but ready to learn. And then she speaks to so many of us when she describes their golden wedding anniversary, painting pictures of when, as married couples everywhere have found, we could be close and intimate and then also that there have been those times when we were alienated from each other, hurting the one we love. We utter words we cannot take back as Nat King Cole sang so hauntingly, but rejoicing yet another time as we found each other again.

I was myself particularly touched by her descriptions of insomnia and Parkinson's disease. None of us are going to live long with all our faculties unimpaired. Many of us know only too well the long nights when counting sheep has been of no avail as we tossed and turned sleepless in the night. How gently and poignantly she writes of the loss of their dear son Steve by drowning, an accident that cut tragically short a life of very great promise.

Those who know Julian of Norwich will be delighted with how Isobel distils some of the best of her Revelations of Divine Love into her poems.

This anthology is a precious gift that we must treasure in an abrasive, cruel world that far too often eschews gentleness, tenderness and love as signs of feebleness. We are deeply indebted to Isobel – a conduit of love and light and gentleness.

Being an artist as well, the poems are illustrated by her charming pictures which enhance the value of the anthology no end.

Desmond Tutu
Archbishop Emeritus of Cape Town

Preface

Writing poetry is something fairly new to me. About fifteen years ago while I was going through a crisis in relationships I found myself trying to express what I was experiencing in poetry. It seemed to flow out of me, consoling me and building up my self-esteem. And so the writing of poetry was given birth. Since then it has been my consolation, my inspiration, my joy. It has also helped me express my faith in new ways. Sometimes it comes easily but more often than not I struggle to find the words, the rhythm, the way to express my thoughts and feelings. Once the words of those first poems were on paper I hesitated to share them, but when I did, others responded positively and encouraged me to share my writings more widely. At the same time I was starting to fulfill a life-long desire to learn to paint.

My background is in science, particularly in Mathematics and Botany. I now started going to art lessons and developed that creative side of myself that had long lain dormant. Art and poetry meshed with each other and in 1999 I put together a small booklet of poems illustrated with line-drawings. I called it *"Something New"* and gave a few copies to friends. Since then I have self-published four other books, each one growing more ambitious, with prayers as well as poems illustrated with paintings or photographs of mine in color, and being more widely distributed. In 2012 a book of meditations on Julian of Norwich, *Making All Things Well*, using my poems extensively was published by Canterbury Press, Norwich, UK, and also by the Paulist Press, New York. Now comes this collection of poems and prayers – again with my illustrations which, with a few exceptions, are from photos or paintings of mine.

The poems are wide-ranging in their style and subject matter – from free-verse to traditional forms, from prayers to light-hearted poems, from poems on nature to poems that ask deep spiritual questions, from poems written when all is light and full of joy, to those that take one into the depths of loss and grief. In short, the poems range between heaven and earth. This collection contains poems from each of the booklets I have put together as well as a number of new ones.

Their setting is South Africa, where I was born and raised, married and in turn raised my own family of two sons and a daughter.

The title also refers to the place where I live, in the *Hemel en Aarde Valley*, the *Heaven and Earth Valley*. It is a beautiful valley not far from the sea, enchanting those who have come across it and rewarding those who live in it. My husband John and I are among those privileged to do so. It was named by Moravian missionaries who, in the eighteenth century, worked in the interior and came to the sea for a rest. They passed through this valley on their way while it was still in its pristine condition, full of fynbos. It has changed greatly since then as first, a colony of lepers, then farmers, settled in its shelter, and now development is taking place at a steady pace.

One of the farms, Volmoed, is now a Christian Retreat and Conference Centre run by an independent Trust. Twelve years ago, when John retired as a Professor of Theology at the University of Cape Town we became part of the Volmoed community. My poetry-writing and my painting flourished. At the same time as we moved I was diagnosed with Parkinson's Disease. I have managed to keep it under control by various means, including prayer and meditation, but rely on medication.

Five years ago, in February, 2010, our elder son, Steve, 48 years old and an ordained minister and teacher of theology like his Dad, a musician and a leader in every way, drowned while riding an inflated tube down a swollen river. We joined the ranks of those parents whose lives have changed dramatically through the loss of a child. I found that expressing my loss in poetry was of help in assuaging the overwhelming grief. Others said they were helped when they read my poems, so I shared them then as I am sharing them now. May they be a blessing to you in your turn.

Isobel de Gruchy
Volmoed,
April, 2015

Notes for the Non-South African Reader

Volmoed (pronounced *fall-moot* and meaning *full of courage*) is the Christian Retreat and Conference Centre where I live with my husband John. It is situated in **The Hemel en Aarde Valley** outside the coastal town of Hermanus, not far from Cape Town. See www.volmoed.co.za

Vermaaklikheid (pronounced *fur-mark-lick-ate* and meaning *jollification*) is a very small village on the banks of the Duiwenhoks River along the south coast of the Western Cape. Together with friends we own a holiday cottage there.

Fynbos (pronounced *fain-bos* and meaning *beautiful bush*) is the fine-leafed shrub-like vegetation of the Cape Floral Kingdom found in the Western Cape. It includes such plants as the proteas, ericas, gladioli, and many other bulbous plants.

Seasons. Remember that the seasons in the northern hemisphere are at the opposite time of year in the southern hemisphere, where spring starts in September, autumn (Fall) in April.

Acknowledgments

For their encouragement from the start, which enabled me to keep on writing, I want to thank John, Jeanelle and Steve, (while he was here to do so), and John and Jeanelle together with Heidi, for reading and commenting on the poems in this collection. For the help I needed in mastering the technology to write down and reproduce my writings, my thanks go to Anton and more latterly to Esther. For encouragement and practical help thanks to Bill Everett, whose ear I bent via the internet a number of times, and to Judy Mayotte, Judy Cooke and Maren Tirabassi for their always positive encouragement. To my friends at Volmoed I am much indebted for enabling me to continue writing and reproducing poetry booklets and for helping to sell them. Finally I offer my thanks to Wipf and Stock for their help in publishing this book and to Ken Leverton at the Methodist Publishing House for making them available and affordable in South Africa.

Between Heaven and Earth

I live in the Hemel en Aarde Valley—
the Valley of Heaven and Earth—
embraced by mountains, a restless river
cuts its way to the sea.
What was it like, this valley,
when it was first named,
before alien vegetation grew rampant,
before the last leopard expired, and the vines,
the roads, the buildings took possession?
What was it like before even that,
when Atta and his people called it home?
Now they would not know it as their own.
Yet it is still the Valley of Heaven and Earth.

It is still here between Heaven and Earth;
between what it was, and what it will become.
And I am here in the same way,
lurching between heaven and earth,
made of the dust of the earth,
yet in the image of God,
feet of clay, but wings of an angel,
earth-bound but heaven-centered,
centered on earth, but bound for heaven,
tottering between the two,
first caught in the grime of earth,
then soaring into the glory of heaven,
yearning, searching for the balance:
to be fully of the earth,
but also fully of heaven.

EARTH

Spring

She does not come boldly,
    and with a firm step,
        sweeping aside the trappings of winter,
but tentatively, tip-toeing in
    with a light touch of color
    or a tantalizing scent,
and then is forced back
    by stubborn winter's last stand.

But she is dancing lightly over the earth,
    teasing us with signs of her presence:
a lightness in the morning
    that the birds sense
    and respond to with song,
a balm in the air
    that draws up the sap
    to swell the buds,
until, one day,
    the sun shines on such a kaleidoscope
    of color and scent and sound
    that we exclaim,
Now Spring is here!

Autumn

Summer slips imperceptibly into
Autumn in Fynbos country.
   not with a blaze of reds and golds,
   but masking its passing with the
mauve of barlaria blossoms,
   the pinks and reds of ericas and
   the fresh new green of protea shoots—
attempting to deceive
   those of us whose roots are in Europe.

Only the exotics; the vines,
   the poplars, the plane trees,
   behave as expected.
Only the sun, hugging more closely
   the northern horizon,
   and lying late in bed
announces Autumn has come.

Approaching Storm

I was aware, could feel it in the air,
could sense it in the pulsing of my blood,
a storm, a mighty storm was on the boil.
First the heat—silent and dense; the sky

Electric blue, the pressure sapping strength.
Now clouds are building, churning, roiling black
as skittish winds riffle the leaves, restless
and disturbing, whispering of blasts to come—

Silencing the birds. It's time to move,
to hurry and prepare, close windows tight,
take washing off the line, secure the doors;
minute and insignificant I feel.

The wind intensifies, the clouds rush on
and threaten to engulf me in a world
alien and dark—a world in which the gods
engage in power-play, with escalating

thunder-growling, lightening-hurling sport.
But unexpectedly the sun breaks through
with startling light—which throws all else into
a deeper dark; I pause and watch entranced,

my eyes drawn to a yellow butterfly
nonchalantly weaving its erratic path
above a buddleia bush. I stop

and stare—all else forgotten in the light,
all else eclipsed by this frail creature's flight.

Afternoon Walk in Winter

I made my way up the mountain path
after a stormy week,
as the sun edged its way behind the ridge.
All was now calm and still,
except for the stream
which was gurgling down the hill
where once the path had been;
cutting out miniature ravines,
dashing over miniature waterfalls,
and pouring into miniature pot-boiling pools.

The stream chattered,
frogs click-clicked from the undergrowth,
a grassbird chirr-chirred its message.
I made my silent way
   up the hill.

Suddenly three hadidas, terrified, it seemed,
by some murderous gang,
took off with their blood-curdling screams,
shattering the silence and my calm.
I stopped and watched them disappear,
then I turned for home,
   and the silence returned.

The stream chattered,
frogs click-clicked from the undergrowth,
a grassbird chirr-chirred its message;
I made my silent way
   down the hill.

Hadidas are also called glossy ibises.
The local frogs are known as "clicking frogs."

All Rivers Flow to the Sea

That all rivers flow to the sea is true—in one sense,
but this river flows to my right as I sit,
and then it flows to my left.
At one time it flows to the sea,
at another it flows from the sea.

The clump of broken reeds that floated downstream
returns floating upstream,
just like the pied kingfisher who flashed past
skimming the water at dawn, will flash past
in the other direction at day's end.
For at this spot the river ebbs and flows with the tide.

How like a river is my mind—
Some thoughts flow straight into the sea:
briefly they appear, flow past and are gone.
Like the pied kingfisher they may return again,
or elusive and showy, they may even settle
on the branch of a tree
long enough to be observed.

Other thoughts, worrying, tiresome, draining,
like broken reeds, endlessly flow past,
disappearing downstream,
only to reappear floating upstream,
when I wish they would be lost forever
in the vastness of the ocean.

But there comes a still point at the turning of the tide,
When there is no movement, no flowing, no change.
Only quiet.
Catch the stillness and hold it to your heart.
It lasts but a moment.

Last Light

The last light of day gilds the hills
with gleaming golden rays,
but not for long.
Here, at this tip of Africa,
there is no lingering dusk.
Without delay
day closes tight her shutters
and it is dark.

Grape Flowers

In the bud the flower,
In the flower, the fruit,
In the fruit, the wine.
In each person, the promise:
always the promise.

May is the Month for Mushrooms

May is the month for mushrooms,
   their soft flesh bursting from nothing into being,
magically pushing through the earth
   in clusters or in fairy rings,
     large orange skirted ones under the pines,
tiny russet ones on rough ground
   aping the pebbles they grow among.

May is the month for mists,
   lying in the valley come morning,
as though the clouds
   had dropped down to sleep off the night,
     and would not now get out of bed.
Then with the day's warmth, they slowly stir
   and lazily rise, allowing the sun's rays
     to pierce them through with golden light.

May is the month for mud.
   As the sun heads north with its heat,
cold winds herd moisture into dark masses,
   until, satiated, they hurl it to the earth
     in fierce squalls of rain,
transforming the dusty paths into
   rivulets and pools of dark, sticky mud.

May is the month for memory.
   The days draw in and the nights grow long,
     leaving only remembrance of
     the perfume and profusion of summer's blooms.
Come September they will return:
   new life from dry seeds or buried bulbs,

but for me there is no return;
my youth was once and is gone.

May is the month for mystery,
  for who can say
    why this should be so.

Ten Thousand Diamonds

The moon sank with unseemly speed—
  a wrinkled burnt orange.
The sun lay in bed, procrastinating
  like a reluctant schoolboy,
while I waited for its warming rays.

Only the wind and I were on the hill—
  and a mournful bird,
till the sun decided to shake off sleep
  and scattered ten thousand diamonds
    on my path.

Robin in the Rain

It was raining,
the rain not falling,
but driven in diagonal slashes
by a cold wind, graying the light,
as it grayed my thoughts.

Till the robin came, handsome fellow,
landed on the bird feeder,
puffed out its chest,
glowing orange-red, and
filled the air with song.

Sometimes a poem is like a caterpillar

Sometimes a poem is like a caterpillar
sitting on a leaf single-mindedly
chomping its way through the succulent greenness,
devouring thoughts and words and leaving
only the unbecoming skeletons of leaf-ribs,
and a plumper, more sluggish self.

Sometimes—does the caterpillar know it,
or does it seem like a death?
The poem emerges from a chrysalis of thought,
shakes itself, pausing to exult in the process,
and lifts off in a flash of fluttering color.

Waterfall

Constantly flowing
as day gives room to night,
which then itself breaks
into a formless world
with light and color.
As sun shines with dry heat,
or is obliterated by soaking rain,
your water flows:
moving, changing,
yet retaining sameness,
replenishing, refreshing
the pool and the river;
constantly flowing
as day gives room to night.

The Orange River Gorge

Hard granite, smooth and unyielding
forms the steep gorge walls,
massive and stark, grey and lifeless,
dwarfing the rushing river far below.

Yet springing to life as the setting sun
lends its color and receives back
vibrant pinks and pearl grays, till
the water too glows with apricot and salmon.

Where the granite yields a mite
a plant defiantly makes its home,
clings to life, shouts the odds and
blossoms in a mad display of purest mauve.

And carried on the upward thrust
of warm embracing air, an eagle glides,
black and awesome, its wing tips threading
the air in effortless exaltation.

We are drawn in, gathered in,
for one short timeless moment.
We drink in the revitalizing scene
and enter that other world
where our flawed humanity
is forgotten.

The Rock Thrush

The rock thrush stood on the rim of the birdbath.
He hopped into the water.
He looked round to make sure no-one was watching.
No-one was, except for me,
watching from behind the window.

He dipped his rump into the water
and shook his body tentatively, splashing water about.
He shook again, more vigorously.
Then he sat up straight and checked his surroundings.

Satisfied he was safe, he hopped back into the water.
His head went under; his body gyrated;
He shook his feathers; he shook his head,
dipping this way and that, with wild delight.

He was dancing to some inner tune.
How like a human he was.
And how joyful I felt
as my spirit joined his dance.

Snake

I had a visitor in my studio the other day.
I came back as the late afternoon sun
angled its heat into the room.
The sliding door was open a fraction
to allow passage of even the slightest breeze.
I was lost in my painting again
when I heard a rustling
from the cupboard near the door.
Then I saw, emerging from the plastic
pushed in on the lowest shelf -
black and sleek, the head of a snake,
followed by another foot or so
of snake. He stopped then.
I found I was standing near the inside door,
ready to flee, but I stopped too.
I watched him—he watched me,
both of us still—he was black and yellow,
surely the wrong color for a boomslang?

Now I thought not of escape
but of capturing his image.
My camera stood ready on a tripod
from earlier—what an opportunity.
Slowly I edged nearer,
slowly switched it on, tilted it, focused
and pressed the button;
and again to make sure.
He never moved,
as though he were posing.

Then I left, shut the door and called John.
We came back and watched
through the glass top of the door.
He was exploring the room,
all two meters of him slowly circling around,
till he found again the gap in the outside door,
silently slithered through and was gone.

Was I afraid, instinctively, yes, at first,
but I felt no panic and no revulsion,
and looking back, like DH Lawrence
seeing the snake at his water trough,
fear and fascination mingled in me,
the instinct to kill warring with my response
to the wonder of his presence,
so that I could also confess
how glad I was that he had come.

I felt no menace, no intention to harm,
but I must confess I am glad that my visitor left
as swiftly and silently as he came.
He was a beautifully patterned creature,
but boomslangs are best observed
from the other side of a glass partition.

A boomslang is a poisonous snake.

The Wasp and the Spider

I saw a large spider on the path.
I didn't mind. It was very dead,
its eight long legs curled up against its body.
Then it was gone.
A small wasp with orange wings
was engaged in a herculean task.
He was reversing up the wall
dragging this spider, centimeter by
muscle-straining centimeter—if
wasps have muscles—behind him.

Hours later, I saw him several meters up
still pulling, still straining upwards.
But alas, he was no Hercules.
When next I looked, he and the spider
had dropped to the ground.
But undeterred he started again.

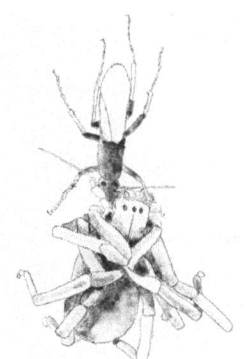

So move over, Robert the Bruce's
web-spinning spider.
Your efforts are child's play.
Give way, Sisyphus. Straining and pushing
your boulder is a piece of cake,
compared to the task of
this tiny orange-winged wasp.

Rainy Morning at the River

Warm air, still and gray,
The river a flat mirror,
Parallel images,

But one glides past,
Carrying leaves, blossoms, reeds,
Slowly out of sight.

The images blur,
The surface pits as rain falls
Gently, silently.

I move my chair,
I long for sunshine, but I know
The earth longs for rain.

Birds come into view
Unperturbed by falling rain.
Why aren't I like them?

They pick at the lawn,
Squabbling, restless, now here, now there.
I watch in silence.

Underlying all
I sense acceptance of what is.
I try to catch the mood.

The Flap of a Butterfly's Wings

Edward N Lorenz: (On Predictability) Does the flap of a butterfly's wings in Brazil set off a tornado in Texas?

Does the flap of a butterfly's wings
       in the forests of Brazil
         set off a tornado in Texas?
Does the swish of a lion's tail
       in the African veld
         set off an avalanche in the Alps?
Does the whisper of a rumor
       over coffee in the office
         set off a storm in the suburbs?
And does an outburst of anger
at the family meal
set off a cloudburst in the community,
       which in turn affects
         every other creature
on the earth?

The Olive Thrush

Shy bird, who named you so?
With orange bill and speckled throat
you radiate a russet chest
under a dark-brown coat.

No olive there. The dove
it is who bears the olive branch,
who courts publicity,
declares its message at a glance.

The window gives me view.
I watch you humbly hop around,
but, startled, flutter out of reach
at any threatening sound.

Only your song cries peace.
You hide from searching eyes and spawn
a merry, dancing lay to thrill
the listener at dawn.

I Walk Alone at Dawn

I tiptoe from the house,
    feeling my way down the still-dark steps.
I sense the day, the place,
    the sun-rise, are mine.
I have opened the door and stepped into
    the mysterious, the secret world
of half-light, of color being recreated
    as yesterday, but as never before,
of birds catching an echo of angel song
    and relaying it to me,
of the wind skipping and dancing
    from leaf to leaf for pure enjoyment,
of light being showered down, seeping into
    each bush and stone and water-surface,
    in turn being radiated outwards
    in escalating brilliance.
I stand and gaze
    and my gazing generates wonder
    and my wonder thanksgiving.
I sigh with satisfaction
    and head on up the hill.

Yellow Daisy

In the midst of death,
like a bright and vibrant flower,
there is always life.

After the Fire

Amidst the burnt-out skeletons of bushes;
Charred and blackened stumps, where
Chalk-white limestone lies exposed and bare,
Flames dancing and weaving in the breeze,
Watsonias, awakened by the heat,
Thrust up their joyous petals and cry,
"Resurrection!"

Well-Spring

This house sat raw on a hillside,
scarred and bare:
an ugly loud intruder.
But it settled down,
flowers grew, the fynbos returned,
birds came to visit—and the porcupine.
Love too was there, so
the house became a home.

Well-Spring is the name of our house

SELF

Who am I?

Am I the person staring at me from the mirror?
Yes, but the surface tells only a part—
There is more hidden behind that stare,
in mind and heart and longing
and seeking and intending,
in skills, in the past,
in the dark recesses
that baffle even me, and
in being part of something wider than myself.

I am a unique individual,
yet I am only who I am
when I am connected,
to husband, child, friend,
fellow Christian,
the wider community,
and most of all to God.

I weave my past—my birthright,
my upbringing, my skills, my interests,
into my now—making a
person, integrated, whole,
vibrant, yet broken,
fragmented, fragile,
on the road still
to being—to establishing who I am.

I am carrying a pocketful of gems
and of stones that may turn into gems.
I travel in hope and in faith,
with love as my guide.

Living in Between

I live in a between time:
   between the promise and its fulfillment,
      between the victory and the mopping up operations,
         between the election and the inauguration.

I live in a between space:
   between earth and air and water,
      between earth and heaven,
         between creation groaning in labor pains
and creation reborn.

I live in a between mode:
   between wretchedness and glory,
      between dark sin and bright goodness,
         between blindness and vision,
falling and rising,
wandering aimlessly and pressing ahead.

And as I live in between,
   my yearning is for God,
      my intention is to wait for him,
for he opens the eye of my understanding.

And when I fail
   and fall again into blindness,
      I will cling to him
         trusting in him to carry me—
In between.

based on Julian of Norwich, Showings, chapter 52.

I am

I am flesh and blood, muscle and bone.
I see, I hear, I taste.
I eat when I am hungry, drink when thirsty,
   take shelter in heat and cold.
When I'm afraid I fight back or run away.

I was nurtured by my parents
   and nurtured my children in return.
I am part of a family, a people, a nation.
I strive above all to survive, and with me
   my children, my family, my people, my species.
I am part of the animal kingdom.

I am a thinker, a problem solver.
I put a name to what I see.
I understand what I hear.
I plan what to eat and drink.
I build my shelter.
When I'm afraid, I decide whether to run away
   or to fight back and how.

I explore how things work
   in order to make life easier and more comfortable
   for myself and my children.
I perceive and think for myself,
   but built on the foundation laid by my family,
   my people, my nation.
I try to work out the why of things, what they mean.
I am *homo sapiens*, a human being.

I am spirit, I am soul,
I know good and evil, truth and falsehood,

beauty and ugliness.
But I struggle to do the good,
   to live the truth, to be beautiful.
My flesh and blood, my need to survive,
   to take care of myself, get in the way.
My reason, my capacity to work things out,
    steer me down the easiest path,
    close down the lid on anything beyond reason.
My experiences, my community,
    prejudice me, hem me in.

But I am made in the image of God.
I yearn for freedom
   to plunge into the depths of my soul,
   to soar beyond the limits of flesh and mind,
   to become one with God,
   to restore fully the image of God in me,
   to become what I am meant to be.
For I am a child of God.

I am what I eat, I am what I see,
   what I experience, what I think.
I am me, but I am my parents, my community,
   my country.
I am me, but I am my children, my grandchildren.
I am me, but I am you, and you are me.
I am what I give you and what you give me;
whether good or evil, true or false, beautiful or ugly.

I am only who I am in relationships,
And only who I can fully be in relationships of love.
I, you, we all together need love above all else,
For the meaning of all is love;

We were formed together in love
And for love.

So we need to grow love, to live it,
give it, accept it, give our life for it.
We need to embrace love with our flesh and bone,
make it the basis of our thinking,
permeate our spirits with it,
and build our communities on it,
For I am, you are, we are together,
citizens of God's Kingdom.

In the Mirror

My Grandma looked old, so old, when I was ten:
gray hair, pulled softly back, framed a wrinkled face,
from which soft gray eyes looked out, gentle eyes,
that welcomed me, enfolded me in peace.

I see her still, each day, now I am old and gray.
She looks out from the mirror, with startled eyes,
with sad, green eyes, with anxious eyes,
that see decline and brace to fight,

and shutter down. I turn away,
denying in my heart what my eyes tell.

The Past

The past is boxed and sealed—
as the dead are sealed in the coffin.
The past has gone as completely
as the water that drained down the plughole.
No good will come of speculating
on the "if onlys," the "might-have-beens":
the future is now a different territory.

Do we carry the box of the past with us,
slowing us down, holding us back,
even walking backwards?
Do we leave it behind,
in the storage room,
refuse to think about it,
go somewhere else,
fresh, devoid of memories?
And if neither one nor the other,
what do we do?

How can we live with it,
but not try to live it again?
How can we let the burden of it go,
but not abandon it altogether?
How can we weave it into
the tapestry of today?
So that remembering inspires, energizes,
so that the sorrow and tears
soften any hardness of heart,
sensitize us to the hurts of others—
Oh, how can we do this?

Go to the Ant . . .

The ant is always hurrying from place to place,
        appearing industrious;
I am the ant.

The squirrel gathers food and stores it,
        sometimes forgetting the place;
I am the squirrel.

The mouse tries to be invisible,
        avoiding the eyes of others;
I am the mouse.

The buck will not fight,
        but flees when she takes fright;
I am the buck.

The hyena lives off what others
        have exerted themselves to obtain;
I am the hyena.

The cat pretends to be obedient,
        while really doing what she wants;
I am the cat.

The snail takes her time to follow her way,
        and quickly withdraws from disturbances;
I am the snail.

The weaver-bird's wife is always critical
        of what the weaver-bird weaves;
I am the weaver-bird's wife.

The fiscal shrike prefers to hunt alone,
        she protects her territory;
I am the shrike.

The goat will be on the wrong side of the divide,
        come Judgment Day;
Am I the goat?

In South Africa a buck refers to an antelope—male or female.

Like a Stalagmite

A stalagmite is built up drip by calcareous drip
and layer upon slow layer, to form a column, strong
and solid, stable in the vicissitudes of life.
It's always there and always growing, but it is
a dead growth, an unchanging growth, becoming in
the end predictable, rigid and unyielding. Tell me
at which point the line is drawn where reliable
becomes predictable, firmness is calcified
into rigidity and standing strong hardens
into unyielding stubbornness. And can I turn
before that point and mould the drip on drip,
the layer on layer in more creative and surprising ways?

Insomnia

There is a hollow in the night
which one can step in unawares
and suddenly all sleep has fled.
There are spirits there that lead
one helter-skelter in a myriad
directions—first one, then another,
pushing into places one would
rather avoid. Then on again
chasing after a task to be done,
a relationship to be mended,
a problem to face.

Where are the tranquil waters,
the Elysian plains, a soothing mantra,
or Morpheus with his soporific balm?
How can one tie up
in a bundle all
skittering thoughts,
fling it to the stars,
and, peaceful now,
descend once more
to sleep?

Fountain

What do you find when you are plunged
into a valley dark as death,
and have to grope your way alone
back into light?

Much pain and tears, confusion, fear,
and hurt that twists into your heart.
Unsure of self, you stay your step.
But is that all?

I found a friend who took my hand
and set me on my way again.
Then I could see along my path
a bleeding wound

Had turned into a fountain that
would feed and germinate a seed
of creativity endowed
with healing balm.

First Kiss

After hearing a song about lost love.

Mostly it lies forgotten,
folded and packed away
at the bottom of the box
marked 'memorabilia'—
my first kiss—

But now I remember—
the surprise of it—
the thrill it gave me—
the way I hugged it to myself—
as I fell in love—

Those first heady weeks
when we 'went out together,'
how they colored my dreams.
But I had to take my leave,
return to university—

He came to the station to say farewell,
promised to be in touch,
kissed me goodbye. . .
stood on the platform watching
as the train pulled out.

It haunts me still -
that image—
and the silence that followed.

Past and Future

. . . he has put a sense of past and future into their minds, . . . Eccl 3:11

I live with my past. I carry it with me,
wherever I go, whatever I do.
It colors my actions, beclouds my sight,
becomes a stumbling block in my path,
                leaving me wounded.

Whenever I try to understand it,
or turn and confront the image I see,
it is protean, changing and re-forming
before my eyes, delusory and elusive,
                slipping from my grasp.

But the sense of the past that God gives me
has redemptive and creative strength,
to transform stumbling blocks to building stones,
wounds to badges of honor and
                barriers to bridges.

So that, as the sense of the future comes
rushing, threatening, into my mind,
a fearful advancing deluge,
I can harness its power as potential
                for growth and not destruction.

Full Circle

As we journey on
we tend to journey back.
Life is not a straight line from start to finish,
like a race, eyes fixed on the tape.
It is more like a circle,
a snake trying to swallow its tail;
the longer the snake,
the easier to touch
the beginning.
Not just Shakespeare's second childhood:
no hair, no teeth,
being led by the hand,
but the mind stretching back,
searching its dark recesses,
remembering, remembering,
sometimes reliving,
hopefully restoring.
The further on we travel
the clearer the view;
the more we see.
Does God grant us this
so that we can grab our tail
and gobble up the regrets,
and the bits that hurt,
and end life complete,
whole, a full circle?

The Milestone Marked Seventy

Funny thing about age—
It's like Janus with the two faces.
The one looking objectively sees each year
with three hundred and sixty-five days
and a set development pattern,
while the one looking subjectively
sees some years lasting forever
and some rushing by;
some being a write-off
and some being a-flood with growth.

And the face of Janus
that looks to the future
sees how long it takes to grow up,
and then how long you're old and useless.
But the face looking back
sees that being old is
being younger than you thought:
that being old is still
full of creative possibilities:
that reaching the milestone marked seventy
is just a pause on the hike
to look at the view.

On Our Golden Wedding Anniversary

We have grown up together, you and I,
acquaintances, friends and then lovers,
teen-agers, eager to spread our wings,
testing the waters and tested by death;
catapulted into instant adulthood.

We have grown together, you and I,
shouldering responsibility, ill-prepared,
buoyed by shared values, shared faith,
dreaming, exploring, risking,
encouraging each other, flying high.

We have grown apart at times, you and I,
going down different roads, absorbed,
excited, leaving the other behind,
but halting, turning, finding one another again,
each growing as we struggled to mend the rifts.

We have grown each other, you and I,
each with our own interests, talents,
urging the other to participate, to learn,
sometimes dragging the other along,
resisting, protesting, but enabling them
to grow—petals unfolding like a flower
touched by the sun's kiss.

We have grown old together, you and I,
by God's grace and love, support,
encouragement each for the other,
by the gift of children, grandchildren, friends,
and we have been tested again by death,
but, because of all that has gone before
we have been able to walk on—together.

The Monster

I dreamt a monster chased me in the night.
I tried to run but he closed in on me.
I faltered, and my body shook with fright.

But as he caught up, to my delight
Drinking a magic potion helped me flee,
I dreamt a monster chased me in the night,

But soon all power was gone, my plight
Was worse, he gleefully could see
I faltered, and my body shook with fright.

I drank more of the potion, but its might
Was spent, and gave such feeble help to me.
I dreamt a monster chased me in the night.

The monster pounced—I woke and it was light
All just a dream, I was relieved to see.
But I faltered still, my body shook with fright.

For still the monster's with me: I must fight—
It's Parkinson's from which I would be free—
This monster still pursues me day and night,
I falter still, my body shakes with fright.

My Prayer as a Person with Parkinson's Disease

My legs and my hands may be shaky,
  but may my courage and
    my faith be firm.
My muscles may become stiff and hard to move,
  but may my mind not become inflexible,
    nor my heart unmoved.
I might lose my balance,
  but may I continue to be balanced
    in outlook and personality.
My hand-writing may become small and squiggly,
  but may I never become small-
    or woolly-minded.
My face may take on a deadpan look,
  but may I always be able to express
    joy, love and peace.
My movements may become slower and slower,
  and may I also become slow to get irritated
    and lose my cool.
My voice may become very soft and croaky,
  but may I not give up on
    communicating with others.
And may I never lose the vital spark
that is me.

OTHERS

Communication

I talk—you catch my words.
You see in them the innuendos
and shared meanings. They hover
a moment and burst into laughter,
caught and volleyed between us.

Another time, and you hear
and do not hear. The words
open the lid on bad feelings,
past hurts, misunderstandings.
These leap out and snap
the cord that binds, leaving
a cold and gaping pit between us.

Reach out, my love, and
grab me quickly before
the gap becomes too great.

You Came into My Life

You came into my life,
touching me,
being part of me
for such a brief moment,
but oh, the abiding imprint
you left on me.

Acrophobia

Why is it that I can stand on the cliff-edge,
lean forward and feel a thrill of awe
as I see the canyon floor far below—
rocks and plants made miniature by the distance,
birds in their flight now beneath me?
Yet this you cannot do.
Some fear holds you back,
some anxiety that says once you get too close
you will have to jump—out into space,
out to your destruction.

Why is it then that you feel the thrill
of a new venture envisioned—get excited
as you stand on the cliff-edge of a new idea,
lean forward to see all you can,
and I hover in the background,
hesitant and anxious, waiting for assurance
that the ground beneath me is firm,
before I step forward to even look?

Friendship

Friendship is the warm sun on a winter's day that thaws our body's chill.
    It is the cool and refreshing rain, bringing the promise of growth.
Friendship is the shelter we run to, finding refuge in a storm.
    It is the gentle push to venture out
        once the storm has passed.

Friendship is the dash of piquant sauce to spice the blandest food.
    It is the wine that turns the dullest meal into a celebration.
Friendship is the joke that brings relieving laughter into a tense situation.
    It is the firm anchor that pulls us back
        when we are drifting into a froth of nothingness.

Friendship is the comfort of firm hiking boots,
    enabling us to climb the rocky mountain.
It is the song of birds and the beauty of flowers
    lifting our spirits as we climb.

Friendship is the tree that keeps growing taller
    and sturdier for a hundred years.
It is the conversation that can be put on hold, and resumed
    as though there were no break.

Friendship is the food that sustains the body,
the book that sustains the mind,
and the spirit that sustains the soul.

A Bunch of Flowers

She had left him—gone to a better life,
so they said, gone where her pain was no more,
so they told him. But she had taken with her
his feelings, his joy, his life.
Now he sat in front of that wooden cask,
with others twittering around, offering comfort,
offering dry and dead words, words of pity
that made him shrink further back into himself—
stony, cold, he sat and stared.

Then he saw that funny old lady, what's her name,
limp up to the front—
what was that intolerable woman doing?
He watched, his mind protesting,
as she bent over and placed
a ragged bunch of flowers
on the floor beside the coffin.
She stood, her head bowed,
then turned to retrace her steps
and he saw her face—grieving and wet with tears.
He shuddered and breathed in deeply,
her grief washing over him, finding cracks,
seeping in and splitting open
his stony defenses—and he wept.

A Death and a Birth

Occasionally there is born a person
who lives a life—not of tedious insignificance—
nor of the selfish pursuit of power and wealth
which leaves others crushed and broken—
but one who lives a life
of triumph over oppression,
forgiveness over revenge
and unity-building over the desire of so many
to divide and control:
a person who, in doing this,
turns his own people's,
in fact the whole world's, denigration,
into adulation and praise.

And we have just witnessed the death of such a person—
Nelson Mandela—
and we have basked in his fame
and claimed him as our own.

Nelson Mandela, who unlike King Canute,
turned back the tide:
the tide of hatred and violence
directed at him and his people,
and turned around the concept
that talking to your enemies
and forgiving them is weakness.

And now we celebrate a birth—
join together around the world to celebrate this birth,
this birth of Jesus Christ—
but why?

Jesus failed where Mandela succeeded.
His life was cut short—
his message terminated.
He died despised in an unknown place—
and yet—and yet,

We celebrate this birth because
it is a fulcrum of history,
the first to turn the tide,
to turn our values on their head.
Mandela embodied it,
as did others,
but so few, so very few.
It needs to be embodied in me, in you
and in each and every person,
because by doing so
we could turn back
the surging tide of evil.

Nelson Mandela died on 5 December, 2013

My Love for You

My love for you never was
a brilliant-hued exotic bloom,
or a heady-scented rose,
never a story to catch the imagination
of the whole world.
Not Iseult loving Tristan,
nor Juliet with Romeo.

More like an acorn,
or the fleshy, round seed
of a yellow-wood,
small and insignificant,
but falling on dark, rich soil
and growing to a mighty tree—
deep-rooted and firm,
stretching arms to pluck
the rainbow from the sky.

Storms may attack with ferocity
and crack the branches,
shredding leaves,
but the tree stands.
Through icy winter,
through darkest night,
through wilting heat,
it will endure,
growing in grandeur
and loveliness.

Is it Love?

I can buy your love,
  but then is it love
    or gratitude or obligation?

I can force your love,
  but then is it love
    or fear of consequences?

I can give you love freely
    and without condition,
then you can spurn what is given
    and turn your back on me,
or you can return what is given
    fully and freely,
        and that is love.

Connections

We know from the song that "your toe-bone connected to your foot-bone,
 your foot-bone connected to your ankle-bone,"
and so on right to the skull.
We know also that each bone is connected to the flesh,
the flesh is connected to the skin,
which is connected to a thousand objects and sensations
in the world outside.

I am connected to you and you to me,
even though I am me and you are you:
We are who we are because
we are connected to each other,
to the outside world,
to all of creation
and to the world within.

As the moon is connected to the earth;
as the river is connected to the sea;
and the towering jagged mountain
to the soft green foot-hills,
so we are connected to them and to each other.

As we walk along the path,
we are connected,
not only to the earth we walk on, but
to where we have come from
and where we are headed.
A book connects us to the world of imagination;
a sacred place to the world of the spirit;
our faith to those who have gone before,
and each play their part in being a mirror
that reflects our image back to us
and to each other.

As the past is connected to the present,
and both weave us into what we are;
as the bread and the wine,
the seed and the fruit,
in connecting, become part of us,
to make us what we consent to become,
the more we cherish our connectedness,
the more we will become our true, unique selves.

The song in the first two lines is "Dem bones, dem dry bones"

I Pray Shalom for You

I Pray *Shalom* for you:
That you wake each day eager to meet whatever comes,
That you look in the mirror and are pleased
   with what you see,
That you accept with courage any limitations
   on your abilities,
That you accept with humility, but develop creatively,
   your special talents,
That you know which things take priority,
That you are not stressed by having
   to set some things aside:
That what you do illuminates who you are,
and that you find joy in all you do.

I Pray *Shalom* for you:
That your face is turned towards God,
That you are secure in the forgiveness of Christ,
That your life is infused with the presence
   of the Holy Spirit,
That your whole being is daily transformed
   and integrated into oneness with Christ,
   and hence wholeness and wellness,
That in having died to self
   you are alive to your true self,
and that love is your prime motivation.

I Pray *Shalom* for You:
That you have a soul-friend to
   accompany you on life's journey,
That you are surrounded by a community
   of support,
That you are a builder of community,

That you are able to transform difficult
   or destructive relationships through love,
That you live in a society that is working towards
   justice, peace and harmony,
And that you may be able to stand strong
   in face of the pain and suffering
     that will inevitably come your way,
         and transform it, for yourself and for society.

I Pray *Shalom* for You:
That the beauty of God's creation enthralls you,
That your love and way of life
   enhance that beauty,
That you do not deplete the resources
   of the earth,
That the rhythm of your life is in harmony
   with the rhythm of others' lives and of all creation,
   so that you become part of God's plan
      of restoration and renewal.

I Pray *Shalom* for You:
That your faith may grow,
That you be filled with love,
and that hope never dies.

When Good Things End

How woebegone we are when good things end.
And end they do no matter how we feel.
The sadness that results can break or mend.

We shared so much with friends, we won't pretend,
Because the joyous times we had were real.
How woebegone we are now at its end.

We were young, naive, and jumped in to defend
The way we set out full of verve and zeal.
The sadness now we feel can break or mend.

The toughest obstacle we could ascend,
The toughest nut with ease could crack and shell.
How woebegone we are now—it's at an end,

For we grow older with each year, we tend
To do that; time keeps snapping at our heel,
The sadness that results can break or mend.

But we're not done yet, let's suspend
All talk of quitting, for this is the deal;
Although we're woebegone when good things end,
Our sadness now won't break, but mend.

Life is Unfair

If life is a game of cards,
some are dealt out aces,
some only twos and threes.

If life is a bowl of cherries,
some are given a plate of plump shiny fruit,
some get handed the pips.

If life is a cruise on the ocean,
some get passage in luxury liners,
some in grubby little steamers that ply the coast.

If the object of life is to make something
out of what we start with,
life is grossly unfair.

Some can easily say they did it their way,
or claim they were master of their fate.
some can only be glad they survived.

We still wait for God to
"bring down the powerful from their thrones,
and lift up the lowly."

And God still calls some out of the top of the pile
and some from the bottom of the pit
to work God's work and be God's co-creators.

The Sprit still moves between and among us
to strengthen and inspire,
like yeast in the dough.

Some can believe this,
take hold of it and find the courage it brings.
Some turn their backs on it.
The choice is theirs.

Inspired by a passage from Flourishing Life, Sandra Levy-Achtemeier, p 21–23, from Julian of Norwich, Showings, chapter 68 and Luke 1:52

A Word Lightly Spoken

A word lightly spoken can drift in the air,
or caught by a breeze like a dry leaf,
it can be blown into oblivion.

A word lightly spoken can hang in the air,
then home in on someone, like a mosquito,
stinging, irritating, making mischief.

A word lightly spoken can exert a power,
a power of its own,
that belies its intention.

My Prayer as I Interact Daily with Others

I see myself as a child of God:
  through being human,
    and then through being a new creature in Christ.
That is my primary identity;
  not nation, family, church, status,
    work, accomplishments, knowledge.
I stand, live, work, have my being in Christ:
  I love with his love,
    think with his mind,
      see with his eyes,
or intend to.
All others are sisters and brothers,
  what they say and do
    does not affect my primary identity.

And so I pray

Lord,
Give me compassion to help when help is needed,
kindness to stand back when help is not wanted,
and help me to see the difference.

Give me openness to share something of my journey if helpful,
humility to listen without talking if that would be more helpful,
and help me to see the difference.

Give me gentleness to ask concerned questions,
reticence to probe intrudingly,
and help me to see the difference.

Give me willingness to organize and advise freely,
patience to hold back if that would be interference,
and help me to see the difference.

Give me courage to be honest in my response if that is called for,
Sensitivity to refrain from honesty if that would be more compassionate,
and help me to see the difference.

Give me reticence to talk about a third person in their absence,
A gentle and loving spirit in which I talk, if it is necessary and helpful,
and help me to see the difference.

Lord,
give me patience when others irritate me, or make me angry,
Help me to see if the cause is with me—
then give me a contrite heart, and the humility to apologize,
if not, give me a forgiving spirit:
but most of all, give me a thick skin.

Lord,
give me a generous spirit;
may I give and receive freely,
not totting up a debit and credit list,
but being sensitive to what is needed and wanted.

Lord,
may I never want more than I should,
more position,
more acknowledgments
more praise,
more of this world's riches,
even more faith than others.
Help me to be content only in your love.

Lord,
Help me to be a peace-maker.
May I be a person who spreads
the mantle of peace over others.
Help me to be gentle without being wishy-washy,

to listen and to understand
and to be an agent of your spirit of unity.

Lord,
may your joy bubble out of me in
lightness and laughter,
but may I always be quick to laugh at myself
and not at others;
to see the humor in a situation
and laugh at it, with others.

But Lord,
even when everything is going wrong
and I feel everyone is against me,
may I not blame others
so that I ignore the faults in me,
may I not blame myself unduly,
so that I sink into despair.;
May I remain faithful
and full of hope.

Lord,
at all times, may my first aim be
to bring glory and honor to your name,
to walk in your way
to grow in your love,
and to play what part I am able to in building up your body.

I ask this in the name and for the sake of Jesus Christ,
my brother, friend and savior,
Amen

Saying the Truth

I want to tell you how I feel.
I want to say I disagree,
to say, in fact, I think you're wrong,
and yet, I always hesitate.

The thing I want to say to you,
now irritates me like the grit
that's worked into the oyster's shell,
but never will become a pearl.

It's much more like the worm that's
growing deep inside the fruit,
that in the end infects the whole.
I want to share this all with you.

The thoughts unspoken are one thing,
but once they're clothed in words,
and then set free upon the air,
how will they come across to you?

I might be free but you are hurt,
and if you are, I can't be free.
I might have just transferred the worm,
so now you feel all rotten too.

They say the truth will set you free,
and always speak the truth in love,
but would it really help to say
that I am right and you are wrong?

So when I see you next I think
I'm really going to tell you now.

the moment comes and then it's gone:
I couldn't let it out somehow.

And so I wonder, is it me—
my lack of courage, or of will?
Or is it that I hear God's voice,
"Just bury this one, let it go."?

Seeing Through a Mist

Watch the mist rise,
   swirling off the water's face.
Its fingers softly drape
   the vegetation in
   pearlescent tulle,
obscuring, mystifying,
   veiling form and
   making all ambiguous.
How often do we think
   we understand someone,
   some action?
Only all the time
   we're looking
   through a mist.

Come Inside With Me

Come inside with me and close the door.
Let's leave the sorrows of the world outside,
And try and find the strength we had before.

We leap-frogged over problems by the score,
We had such self-assurance then, and pride,
Now come inside with me and close the door.

When evil punched and knocked us to the floor,
Up in a thrice, no slacking in our stride:
Can we still find the strength we had before?

But, older now, and punch-drunk, tired and sore,
It seems that evil holds sway, far and wide,
So come inside with me and close the door.

I feel, when down, I stay down more and more,
Can I be revitalized, and turn the tide?
And really find the strength I had before?

The one who gave you life will all restore,
Will walk with you and be your friend and guide,
So draw aside with me and close the door
Indeed we'll find the strength we had before.

Dream World

At the gathering of friends she saw him.
Even after the passage of so much time—
even though her face was now haloed with silver,
even though she was glad the relationship had ended,
she watched him with eager eyes
and felt the carpet of the years roll out, running
down the steps to link them together again.
Then he saw her and smiled,
a smile that healed the neglect of years
as they moved towards one another.

A voice called out his name, and he turned.
A younger woman came running into his arms
and she could read passion in their kiss.
She no longer mattered. She no longer existed.
She watched, a deep sadness seeping into her being,
not from the renewal of their relationship no longer possible,
but from feeling cast off; as of no account.
She was a bystander in the drama of life.

And then she woke.
It had been but a dream.
Yet the sadness remained.

Alfred Mxhalisa

The psalmist tells us that the man
who does not tread the sinner's path,
but delights in the law of the Lord,
shall be happy.
He is like a tree planted by a water-course
that flourishes and bears fruit.
He prospers in all he does.

Alfred Mxhalisa was just such a man.
He was a good and righteous man—
He walked in the way of his Lord.
But he did not prosper.
He struggled in all he did.
His wife succumbed to alcohol.
His only son changed from a child full of laughter
to a shadow of a man full of addictions.
His daughter of promise was struck by mental illness.
He was poor. He lived in a miserable house.
Circumstances shut the door on any opportunity
that tried to knock.
Yet he was a good and righteous man—
He never wavered from walking in the way of his Lord.
He was loved and respected,
but he did not prosper.

He was a man of faith,
even when ill health dogged his way,
even when it took his life.
Was he a happy man?
Not as the psalmist predicted—
Not seemingly to us.

But his delight was in being faithful
and walking in the way of his Lord.
Surely he is prospering now.

*Based on Psalm 1, reflecting on the life of Alfred Mxhalisa
who lived in Vermaakilkheid.*

Struggle Tapestry

"What did you do in the struggle, Dad?
What did you do in the struggle?"

I added but a stitch or two to the tapestry,
the tapestry woven in a rainbow of colors,
a wealth of stitches, some stained in blood;
the tapestry growing more complex, more varied,
over many years; a picture emerging of freedom,
community; a vision of what could be,
as each person, outstanding or of little significance,
added their own unique offering.

I added my stitch or two, and the tapestry
would not be diminished if I had not.
But I would. And as the work was hung
for all to see, I was glad that my few stitches
were part of the whole.

Walk On, Walk On.

Walk on, walk on, into the unknown way,
Dark though it seems with obstacles and fears.
God will direct your steps both night and day.

The path winds up a mountain steep and gray,
The green and pleasant way quite disappears.
Walk on, walk on, into the unknown way.

You're all alone. You find no-one will stay.
All you have left are memories and tears.
God will direct your steps both night and day.

But now some friends walk at your side and they
Will help you bear the burden of your cares.
Walk on, walk on, into the unknown way.

Tempted to take it easy and delay,
You may imagine God no longer hears,
But still he directs your steps both night and day.

And there are also times of joyful play,
And celebrations as years follow years.
So walk on, walk on, into the unknown way.
Let God direct your steps both night and day.

*First written for our granddaughter Thea's
21st birthday, not long after her father died.*

Looking Right Through

I can look through a window
and see the view beyond,
without seeing the glass,
because that is the nature of windows.

But when I met her after many a moon,
she greeted me and looked right through me.
Maybe the view beyond was worth seeing,
but it is not my nature to be a window.

I can be transparent.
Transparency is very PC at the moment,
but that means showing the real me—
not hiding behind shutters.

But she looked right through me.
I was not there. Was I ill, was I well?
What was I doing with myself?
She did not care enough to ask.

Being regarded as a piece of glass
diminished me. I could feel
myself getting louder as I tried
to be visible. Then going silent

as that made no difference—
felt resentment, hurt, anger.
Then she moved on,
leaving me yearning for affirmation.

Endings

It is a time for endings,
a time for closing the door
on a worthwhile activity,
a time for saying goodbye
to a precious friend.

Doors close but not for good.
New doors will open on
new ways of service, and,
though far, the friend is still a friend.

But how to handle doors that
shut for good with age;
the end of independence,
the end of using our skills?

God give us courage even then
to look for new doors to open,
even if the door shuts on the
grave of the one we love.

FUN

Ode to a Frenetic Old Lady

Dear Lord, I should be slowing down,
I should be easing out
Of all the tasks I'm slaving on;
That keep me running all about,
              That should be done.

O Lord, I seldom sit and rest,
I seldom meditate.
At my age, sitting hands on chest,
I all my time should dedicate
              To just that quest.

Yet these pursuits keep pulling me
In different directions,
Sewing, writing, art, enthralling me
Like feverish infections
              Over all of me.

I long for a spell of quiet time,
But then I find I'm bored.
I need some task for hand and mind,
I guess we know by now, Dear Lord,
              That's how I am.

Confabulation

The mind when at a loss confabulates
And story, myths, as reason, it creates.

Contrary Creatures

We are
by far,
contrary creatures;
for one of our features,
is that when it is hot,
we wish it were not,
and when it is cold,
if truth be told,
we wish it were hot.

Going Uphill

Walking up the steepest incline,
Puffing as I make the effort,
Said to keep me fit and supple,
As if that could be a comfort.

Rain Storm

The heavens opened and it rained
The wind its staunch ally,
It did not fall from heaven to earth,
But horizontally.

The brolly was of no darn use,
It just blew inside out,
I soon got soaked from head to foot,
My inside to my out.

Time

I can feel the sand is pouring
Through the unforgiving hourglass.
Once it's through there's no returning.
Use it well before it's passed.

Saturday at Gran's

Saturday is here again.
Means I go to see my Gran,
In the car, stay for lunch,
Eight-year-old is pleased as punch.

Welcome at the kitchen gate,
Smells waft out, I cannot wait
To go in, play my part,
Baking pasties and a tart.

Table much too high for me,
Stand on stool so I can see,
Given lump of pastry dough,
Rolling pin and off I go.

Rolling back and forth at length,
Leaning hard with all my strength
Doesn't do the dough much good,
Lightest touch is what I should.

Fill the dough with 'tatoes, meat,
Crimp the top with fingers neat.
Couldn't get the way to do it.
Mostly I just went and blew it.

Still my Gran cares not a jot.
Into oven goes the lot.
Out come steaming, golden pasties,
Devour for lunch, so hot and tasty.

My grandparents were from Cornwall, where pasties are traditional fare.

Taking a Hike

Men walk to get there:
talking intently of something else,
 striding forward;
   the faster, the steeper,
     the harder, the better.

Women walk to experience the way:
What is that flower?
 Did you see the robin?
  The proteas look wonderful.
    and, Just look at that view!

The Second Try

God made Adam from the earth.
God molded, formed and gave him birth.
God took one look and said, "Oh, dear!
I made a mess of that, I fear."

God took a rib and tried again,
And vowed perfection to attain.
Eve emerged to God's delight,
"I know this time I've got it right."

The Lecture

We wait expectantly,
animated, the room buzzing,
small groups talking;
people arriving, greeting
one another, finding seats,
till "May I have your attention,"
arrests the flow.
The room gradually grows quiet.
The lecture begins—
we listen—
time moves on.
The lecture continues;
we look for value, for meaning,
we look for anything
to re-animate us—
we stop listening.
We look at the clock,
we move our feet,
we look around—
time slows—
we wait
for it
to end.

Procrastination

Procrastination is the thief of time,
But waiting till the right time is no crime.

Whale-Watching

Eight of us went out one day,
To see if we could catch some whales,
We knew that they were in the Bay,
And sure to show their tails.

We turned our binocs on the scene,
While John called, "There was one!"
We only saw where they had been,
Of sight of them was none.

We stood and leant against a wall,
While peering out to sea:
The eighth got tired of it all
And sat down, that was me.

Then John said, "Let's go nearer,
Get closer, where they are."
We thought that was a good idea,
He went to fetch the car.

We drove to Kraal Rock round the Bay,
And there close to the shore,
Were two, three, four large whales at play,
Who would have asked for more?

We watched in fascination,
They breached and splashed and dived,
We felt exhilaration,
And very much alive.

We took with us our memories,
Our photographs as well,
Eight people satisfied with these,
And stories still to tell.

To the Little Mouse

Oh, little mouse, please stay outside—
The outside, wild and free is yours,
And even if you try and hide,
You'll cop it if you come indoors.

You come inside and eat our food,
You chew up books to make your nest,
I don't think you have understood,
That you are just a down-right pest.

I am sorry but I must
Insist you leave my house at once,
And if I find you here, I'll just
Give you to the cat for lunch

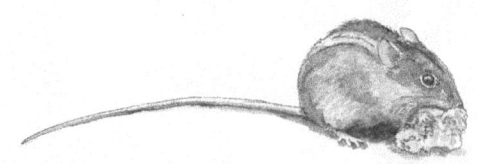

GOD

Morning Praise

Praise be to you, Lord God,
Creator of all,
in whom we came into being, exist,
and to whom we long to return,
as to a mother, who stands
with arms outstretched waiting
to pull us into her embrace.
Lead us, guide us, keep us.

Praise be to you, Jesus Christ,
son of the Father,
who lived and died for each one of us,
and who is alive in us now.
Let us walk with you today.
Restore us, renew us, and heal us.

Praise be to you, Holy Spirit of God and Christ,
who lives within and between us,
who empowers us,
and shows us the way.
Fill us, teach us to pray,
transform us and make us whole.

Praise be to you,
Holy Trinity of Power and Wisdom and Love.
Be in us and we in you today,
and for each day yet to come.
Amen

Based on the writings of Julian of Norwich

God in a Point

" I saw God in a point," Julian of Norwich, Showings, Chap 11,

God always was: the earth was not.
At a certain point in time, the earth came into being.
God was in that point—
God was in the coming into being of the earth.

God made all that is made.
God does all that is done.
All that is made points to God.
All that is done points to God.
God is the point of it all.

Why did God make our earth?
Was there a point to it?
God made it for love.
Love is the point of it all.

At the centre of a sphere is a point.
The sphere may revolve—the point is still,
stable, secure; holding it all together.
Our earth-sphere revolves.
It whirls around, spinning on its axis:
At the centre, a still secure point.
God is in that point.
God is that point.

Tree in the Desert

"They are like trees planted by streams of water." Ps 1:3a
"And the leaves of the trees are for the healing of the nations." Rev 22:2

A tree planted by streams of water
flourishes—soaking up easy sustenance,
spreading its luxurious canopy.
Consider then the camelthorn,
shouting defiance from its arid dwelling,
skeletal and brittle in the dry and dusty winter.
It does not wait for the first rains of spring,
but, stretching deep for hidden moisture,
bursts prematurely into its green filigree of life:
Symbol of hope for the promise of rain to come.
Surely *its* leaves will be for the healing of the nations.

The camelthorn or kameeldoring is an acacia tree of the African bushveld

Abraham's Call

He felt so restless, could not settle down.
A puzzling notion kept on coming back,
planting the thought that he should leave his home.
No voice, no clarion call, no startling dream,
just a feeling, an idea, preposterous and strange.
It niggled and nagged, obtrusive as an aching tooth.
Then, gathering power, like a freak wave
it swept away all satisfaction with what was,
and he knew he must set out to go,
he knew not where and find, he knew not what.
But looking back across the years,
seeing what he had done,
he knew the call had been from God
and he knew God.

Mystery and Meaning

What does it mean—this life of ours?
No meaning, only mystery:
From stars to mountains, lakes to flowers,
Psychology to history,
For each to understand their story,
Take it on trust, what comes, what's past,
All will make sense one day, at last.

No-one Knows my Name

I am the girl that no-one's heard of,
no-one remembers, no-one cares,
no-one even knows my name.
Could it be that I never even lived?
Yet that far-off day seems more real
now than many another.

Early spring light, soft and pink as I opened the shutters,
was suddenly shadowed by the imposing form
of a stranger—tall and serious.

"Greetings—the Lord is with you."—
And, seeing I trembled,
"Don't be afraid, I have a message for you.
You will bear a son, and he will inherit
his father David's throne."

I stood still as a statue, while my thoughts
whirled and jangled—I was not married.
I was too young. It must be a joke.
Who was this man anyway?
Was I really hearing this word, or imagining it?
He stood waiting and I cried out, "Oh no!
I'm not the one, don't ask me!
There must be someone else."
The light in his eyes dimmed with a look,
not of vexation surely, but of deep sorrow.

You know, don't you, where he went?
And that is why no-one knows my name.

Christmas Morning, 2009

Radiating out from the centre,
as yet below my line of sight,
the clouds fan out,
thin and insubstantial, grey and lifeless,
until they begin to catch fire;
from the centre glowing red,
iridescent orange, now alive with light,
the outer rays softer with gentle pinks,
cerise and violet:
the extraordinary breaking through
the ordinary dawning of the day.

An ordinary couple, having made a journey,
forced on them at an inopportune time,
arriving to find inadequate accommodation,
with her birth pains starting,
and, after all the usual effort and messiness,
laboring through the night-time hours,
a boy is born:
the extraordinary breaking through
the ordinary in the birth of this child.

In Remembrance of Her

Mark knew the story,
the story of how the woman poured
her perfume over Jesus' head,
how those sitting at table were shocked,
how an angry murmur rose and
crescendoed into a righteous protest—
"Just think how many poor could have been fed,
in place of this wanton and wasteful act!"

And how Jesus, not angry, not embarrassed,
but touched to tears, looked at her,
looked at the men, his close companions,
and said, "You still can't see it, can you?
You have walked with me for so long,
and you still can't see it,
but she understands,
she knows what I must do—
she has anointed my body for burial,
and wherever my story is told
this story will be told
in remembrance of her."

Mark knew the story;
and told the story
in remembrance of her:
But in remembrance of who?

Based on the story as told by Mark in Mark 14:3–9

Good Friday on Mauritius—A Prayer

How can I travel through time and space,
from the lush green of this island
   to that harsh and arid land,
from this safe and tranquil dawn
   to the menacing clamber of that day,
from this turquoise and azure light,
   to that eerie darkness suddenly enveloping the land,
from the soft cooing of the doves
   to that two-fold strident cock-crow?

How can I remove myself
from the bottomless cokes and cappuccinos
   to that sponge of sour vinegar proffered
   on a branch of hyssop,
from the carefree peals of children's laughter
   to the vulgar jests of sadistic soldiers,
from the twinge of muscles aching from pulling
guide-ropes and tow-ropes,
   to the agony of nails driven through hands and feet,
from living life to the full,
   to life-blood slowly ebbing away?

How can I travel, Lord, through time and space,
   from this my world to yours
   and stand with you—even for a brief moment—
   at the foot of the cross?
Lord, I want to be there with you:
   help me to do so.

Good Friday, 2011, on Mauritius

Easter Morning, 2009

I have lived through seventy years:
seventy springs and my own spring,
season of buddings and new growth;
seventy summers and my own summer,
full growth, green and vigorous;
seventy autumns and my own autumn,
season of fruitfulness, late growth, consolidating;
seventy winters and my own winter,
shedding, letting go and resting.

I have lived through seventy Easters:
seventy times the story retold,
the agony and horror of the cross,
the despair of the disciples till
Sabbath morning,
when the women come to the tomb.
Seventy times—no surprises,
I have heard it again and again.

But somehow, in some way,
this story is still new—seventy times new, alive, fresh,
breaking into our old, tired, despairing world—
Christ is risen! He is risen indeed!
Christ is risen! Seventy times risen!
Seventy times seven risen!
Risen and alive and with us, each one,
for seventy years or forty-eight,
or fifteen or eleven:
dying and risen for us
and with us forever.

Easter Morning, a Year Later

Now I have lived through Easter once again,
number seventy-one—and the hardest—
for death has visited the family,
snatched one of us away—
left us reeling, tottering, shattered,
and there is no resurrection—
he has gone for good.
Can the message, "Christ is Risen!"
lift me up, and sustain me?
Help me to go on living day by day
towards my seventy-second Easter?

8 May, 2010, at Vermaaklikheid with the family

Sonnet to Silence

Into the silence cloaking me around,
into the overarching solitude,
the stillness of this early morning hour,
I step with quiet confidence and trust.
I bring myself, my thoughts, my fears, my hopes,
the rushing, tumbling chaos of my mind,
the burdens of a busy yesterday,
the pressing choices that await today.
I sit, I wait; I yearn to hear you speak
out of the silence cloaking me around.

Jacob's Ladder

The ladder stretches to heaven,
rung upon rung, upright, hard.
Luminous angels, ascending, descending,
effortless, lighting the steps.

How to ascend, when, head
on a stone, body in dust, Jacob
shrinks into himself, pulls his cloak
defensively tighter, wanting

to make his shame, his deceit, himself,
invisible. How to pull himself,
thus burdened, step by painful step,
up, up, forever towards heaven.

But the Lord stands beside him,
feet on earth, touches him,
accepts him, blesses him,
promises to journey with him,
though he deserves none of this.

Jacob Wrestles with God

The dark night drew its somber cloak around
A man whose look conveyed an equal dark,
That filled him to the depths with seething dread.
He thought of flight; but still he stood his ground.

And then he could not flee, for someone strong
Had caught him in a grip and he fought back.
They wrestled there, those two, but who was this?
His hidden past, the dark side of himself?

And back and forth and down and up all night,
For Jacob would not slack until he came
Right through to resolution and was blessed.

A new day saw a new man stand up tall.
Injured, but whole, ready to face what came,
For Israel had won, but so had God.

Can you Hear Your Name?

Listen, can you hear your name being called?
It echoes off the hills and valleys,
   always there, unchangeable.
It whispers from the bursting buds,
   newly formed in fresh beauty.
It persists through your grief and tears.
It resonates through your restlessness.
Calling, calling—
   as a walker calls her dog who has run off,
   as a mother calls her child who has wandered.

For you were made to be one with God, your maker;
   strong and unchangeable as the hills;
You were given new life by Jesus, your Mother, your Brother;
   as the spring has brought new life to the flowers.
For he has known grief;
he has known trouble and discontent;
he has known disappointment and loneliness.

Listen, can you hear your name being called?
   Come into those arms waiting to hug you;
     Come home where you belong.

Based partly on Julian of Norwich, Showings, chapter 58

Confession

Lord, I have seen again my real self,
the self that hides behind the facade of graciousness,
the self that sets standards for others,
that looks at people from a haughty
self-righteous position and sees
what is not right in them
according to those standards,
the self that passes judgment,
clothing it in concern for their well-being,
but just being mean or unthinking,
or trying to be superior and clever.

Lord, I have seen again my real self
and I don't like what I see.
You see that real self too—
look with compassion,
be merciful and forgive me—yet again.

You see my short-comings, my self-interest,
my willful desire to follow my own way,
my lack of love.
Help me to see it in myself too, Lord,
before I even think, open my mouth or act,
And having seen, help me to change,
so that my real self may become more like you.

Amen.

The Trees of Life

A tree at our beginning:
a tree in a garden,
that brought us all knowledge,
and with it struggle and strife.

A tree along the way:
a tree of shade in the day's heat.
It became a tree of
hospitality and promise.

A tree at the centre:
a tree on a bare hill,
stripped of all beauty
and full of suffering.
It brought us salvation.

A tree at our ending:
a tree on the banks of a river.
Its leaves will be
for the restoration and healing
of all people.

Lord God of Power and Wisdom and Love

Lord God of power and wisdom and love,
  Creator and sustainer of all that exists,
    Yet close friend and lover of each one of us,

Give us an awareness of your presence,
  For we cannot see you clearly.

Open our eyes to see you in your glory,
  And in your suffering on the cross,

Open our ears to hear you calling our name,
  And to listen to your instructions for us, each one.

Guide our feet on the right path,
  And fill the very depths of our being with your love.

In Jesus' name,
  Amen

*Based on Julian of Norwich's
concept of the Trinity*

Prayer for the New Year

God, our Creator, you set the universe in space,
galaxies, planets, stars,
swinging endlessly in their set orbits,
turning, hurtling, circling,
bringing into being darkness and light,
giving us night and day;
heat alternating with cold, growth with dying,
giving us seasons.

But we made the year:
we decreed that this day,
this day we call the First of January,
this day, shall be the first in a new cycle of days,
It will start a New Year.

So God, as we turn from the old year that is passing,
help us to turn from all its pain,
leaving deep sorrow and anguish behind.
Help us to close the door on its hurts,
shutting off anger and resentment.
Help us to leave behind its failures,
taking no shame or blame with us.
But enable us to take with us
the new insights, ways of seeing and being
all of these have taught us.

As we turn the page
and step into the new chapter of a new year:
all up ahead, unknown, open and beckoning,
help us to carry with us
all the good, the love, the support,

the strength, the grace,
that was given to us in the old.
And may this day;
this arbitrary day,
made special by us,
be blest by you,
God of all time,
of day and night,
seasons and years,
the Alpha and the Omega.
Be our companion and guide
on the journey ahead.

Keeping the Silence

How can I settle the silence
solid and still in my heart,
so that the world's noisy discourse
does not sweep it away, while
sucking me down in its vortex,
spinning me round and around?

How can I learn to be still,
centered and stable, secure,
silence my voice, stop my tongue,
open my ears to just listen
open my heart to receive:
radiate stillness around?

We Do Not Know

"You do not know now what I am doing, but later you will understand.,"
John 13:17

"If in my name you ask me for anything, I will do it.,"
John 14:14

Lord, we do not know—
there are so many things we do not know—
so many "whys" and "what fors"
so many dark mysteries in our lives
where we are waiting for a light
to be switched on
so that we can see and understand.

We do not understand about death—
yes, we know we must all die,
but why the young?
Why do our sons die so young? Our daughters?
Why do husbands, wives, fathers, mothers die,
it seems before their time,
leaving the aching gap of what was
and the emptiness of what might have been?

We do not understand about evil,
how it is conquered, yet still wields such power.
We do not understand your promises;
you promised that if we ask
anything in your name, you will do it.
We so often ask for good things in your name,
and so often we do not see you do it.

Lord, we do not know now what you are doing.
All we can do is to walk on,
And pray that you will walk with us,
And that some day we will understand.

Was it Easy for You, Jesus?

We want to think it was easy for you,
easy to grow up in Nazareth,
easy to know what was right
and just as easy to do it:
easy to love others,
the lovely and the unlovely.
Yes, we know you were a human—fully,
but you were also fully God.

Were you ever selfish with your toys?
Did you ever take the biggest piece of cake?
Did you hit your little brother when he annoyed you?
Did you talk back to your mother in a smart-ass manner?

Did you disappear for hours on end,
making her sick with anxiety?
Oh yes, we know you did—for days in fact,
and then you had a slick answer ready.
But did that make you feel good?
Did it change the view
of what was right and wrong for you?

Was it easy to always be obedient to your father?
And when it came to the choice of
heavenly father over earthly,
how easy was that?

We want to think it was easy for you,
because then we have an excuse
for making such a mess
of our own choices,
because we find it so hard.

Made in God's Image

If God created man in God's image
and made them male and female
and God is one—surely so are they.
And God is Trinity—three equal beings
in relationship, yet one—surely so are they.
None dominates, the Father gives
glory to the Son, the Son works through
the Spirit, the Spirit honors the Father.
why is the image so skew, so unequal in us?

And if we are made in God's
image—male and female—surely so is God.
He is she in equal part,
he is Mother, She is Father.
Why do we settle for only half of God,
ignoring the other?

God, complete your image in us,
help us to see the whole of you.

Be Perfect

"Be perfect," said Jesus,
    "as your heavenly Father is perfect."

Perfect?
    A crucified God,
Perfect?
    With wounds tearing open his hands and feet;
    with a gaping hole in his side,
Perfect?
    A God who falls victim to the machinations
    of his political and religious enemies.
What sort of perfect God is that?

Is it the God who has perfected
the way of taking the pain,
    the wounds,
       the scars of life
          and transforming them through love,
Perfectly?

Based on Matt 5:48

We Need Easter, Lord

Lord, I see the beauty of your world,
the sparkling turquoise of the sea,
the solid mass of the mountains,
the fragile loveliness of a flower,
and I can praise you.

But there is that other ugly world
that frightens me—
it overwhelms me, renders me helpless:
that world where people are prisoners to poverty.
Violence and misery mark the measure of their lives,
they trudge an endless treadmill
without a break—to stop is to fall off
into worse—a dark and bottomless pit.

I can't bear to hear about it, to think about it.
I don't know how—do I even care enough?— to act.
Lord, it is Good Friday—bad Friday—writ large,
Bad Friday, Black Saturday, repeated
endlessly, like the treadmill.

We need Easter, Lord,
send Easter!—to the city's slums
to the shacks, to the shebeens,
to the country's desolation,
to the hearts and minds and wills of all.
Break upon our world with Easter.
Break open our world with Easter.

Easter 2013

A shebeen is an unlicensed drinking shack in the townships

For Rachel's Children

Jer 31:15   Rachel is weeping for her children;
she refuses to be comforted for her children,
because they are no more.
vs 17a   there is hope for your future, says the Lord.

For all of Rachel's children, weep, oh weep,
Because we see in shock they are no more.
There is no comfort for our grief is deep.

This time a gunman came and with one sweep
Of bullets twenty children hit the floor.
For all of Rachel's children, weep, oh weep.

Some children find their life is held so cheap,
They're bought and sold like goods are in a store.
There is no comfort for their grief is deep.

Some, day by day, go hungry off to bed,
Whole households run by youngsters not much more
Than children, just like Rachel's, weep, oh weep.

The education that should help them leap
Up to a better life is bad at core;
There is no comfort for our grief is deep.

God's promised hope—do we believe he'll keep
His word and countless blessings on us pour?
For all of Rachel's children, weep, oh weep;
We hope for comfort, yet our grief is deep.

After the shooting of children in a school
in Newtown, Connecticut, 14 December, 2012

Massacre, Nairobi, 21 Sept 2013

Oh Lord, Lord, our hearts are aching,
for widows are keening,
devastated, inconsolable,
their husbands have been snatched from them,
their children's father, the family's bread-winner.
And husbands are weeping for their wives,
parents for their children
and children for their parents.
Over sixty men, women and children gunned down:
their sin, being where they were when they were—
fodder for a cause, pawns in a ruthless plan,
objects slain to make a point.
More than sixty men, women and children killed:
and one, our friend,
in a foreign land giving of himself,
till a bullet made him give his whole life.

Oh Lord, Lord, we are keening too,
devastated, shattered, full of questions:
Why all this senseless killing?
Where were you, Lord?
Why does evil have such power?
Why do your people suffer so?
We know there are no answers,
yet we can't stop asking,

Will you come—
to support the widows,
console the widowers,
care for the orphans?
Will you help us to keep on
believing that no matter what,
all will be well?

HEAVEN

The poems in this section were written after our son, Steve, drowned on February 21, 2010. He was 48 years old, a father, husband, son, brother. He was a theologian like his father and making a valuable contribution to the faith in his work for development, the poor, and justice.
The poems are arranged chronologically.

All Shall be Well, after Death?

When the ordered tenor of our life
is shattered by the unimaginable,
when the phone-call that splinters
others' lives rings for us,
when a nightmare that horrifies
turns into reality,
how can we believe that
anything could be well again—
ever?

Anguish breaks over us in torrents,
like the torrents that overwhelmed you—
submerged you, extinguished your life:
but we surface again,
we go on living,
we face each day,
wounded and grieving.

We hold on to each other,
and take a halting step.
Can we dare hope that
all shall be well,
and all shall be well,
and all manner of things shall be well again—
ever?

This was written for and read at a service on 4 March 2010, in Steve's honor at Volmoed.
Quoting Julian of Norwich: Showings, chapter 32

Dawn will Come

Slowly, steadily, silently,
   the dawn light creeps up the hill.
Slowly and silently, being disturbed,
   the buzzard rises from the clump of bushes,
     and floats down the incline
as the light gathers the whole spectrum
   into itself, and changes from red,
     through yellow, to colorless white.
The wind is silent.
The birds are silent.
A haze hangs over the fields,
   muting the vegetation—
     it echoes my heart.
Here dawn will come—
   as surely as it came yesterday,
     but to my heart?

March, 2010

Is Death only slipping through the door?

It has been said that "Death is nothing at all,
I have only slipped through the door
into the next room"—
    but what help is that to us,
    for the door is firmly shut,
    and there is no coming back?
"Those who believe shall never die"—
    but what help is that to us,
    for they do, really?
they are no longer with us,
    to fetch the kids,
    to pay the bills,
    to call and say Hi!

Even if "Death is nothing at all,"
    and the dead live
    and see us and know,
    from that next room,
what help is that to us,
    who wake on this earth,
    and go about our daily tasks
    with a black hole in the middle
    of our world?

17 March, 2010

The first 3 lines, which are well know, are from a sermon preached by Canon Henry Scott-Holland following the death of King Edward VII of Great Britain in May, 1910.

Easter Message, 2010

My ears hear words
   to which my mind responds —
   words that I have long accepted,
   but my heart now shuts them out:
"Jesus Christ is Risen!"
"Death has been conquered,
   has been swallowed up in victory!"
"Death has lost its sting!"

My heart knows that death
   still has the power to yank
   the carpet of every certainty
   from under my feet and leave
   me in desperate disarray.
My heart knows that death still stings,
   still explodes like a bomb into my life
   and changes everything forever.
My heart knows that in the midst of life
   there is death—
   murder, violence, accidents, disease,
   earthquakes and floods:
But must death have the last word?

Can I look from the heap of rubble
   where I am lying
   and see life?
Are there arms reached out to lift me up?—
   Someone to say
   "Walk on, I am with you.
In your weakness, rely on my strength—
   it is sufficient for you.
Hang in there—for nothing—not even death,

    can separate you from God's love—
Hang in there—till your heart
    can be open to hear."
And hang in there I must—
    for who else has the words of life?
Hang in there I will—
    O God, help me.

Easter, 4 April, 2010

I'm OK, I'm Alright

I'm OK meeting people at a party,
even when they greet me with a special hug
and ask, "How are you doing?"
and I answer, "I have my ups and downs,"
not knowing what else to say.
I'm OK when their son makes a speech
at their Golden Wedding Anniversary.
I'm OK—until I realize you will not be there
to do that for us
in your own inimitable way.

I'm alright listening to music,
even nineteen-seventy's folk-singers—
or in church, singing hymns.
I'm alright listening to young people singing,
even the young man singing with his guitar.
I'm fine—until it crosses my mind

that I will never hear you do that again,
in the special way you had.

I can cope with reading about your achievements—
your academic prowess, your ability to organize,
your penchant for tackling difficult issues
or people, with equal dexterity.
I can cope with reading of your zaniness and humor,
I can cope—until I read about how,
with compassion, you spent time with a young man
in serious trouble and gave him opportunities
to make something of his life.
I can try to be unmoved—until the thought overwhelms me
of how you really cared for the underdog.

I can manage talking about Vermaaklikheid
and planning to go there again,
knowing that I must.
I can manage, hearing about the discussions
to control development,
even thinking and talking about what needs doing
in our house and garden.
I can manage, looking at photos
of all the family having fun together,
even photos of you.
I can manage—until I try to picture all of us being there
without you.

April, 2010

You will not be Overcome

In my deep distress, O Lord,
I turned to your promises;
I shouted them to you;
I flung them back at you:

   "The Lord protects you;"
   "The Lord will deliver you,"
   "No evil will befall you,
     for his angels will bear you up
      so that you do not dash your foot
      against a stone."

I clung to these, O Lord,
but there was no protection;
no deliverance—no angels
to lift our son up—only the stones
dashing his head—the waters covering him ,
death claiming him.
   What about your promises—
     O Lord, where were you?

Then I remembered those other promises—
promises that Jesus made:
    "The gate is narrow and the way hard."
    "You have a cross to carry daily."
    "The world may hate you."

For he did not say,
"You will not be tempted,
You will not be troubled,
You will not be distressed."
But he did promise,
"you will not be overcome."

No easy ride, no special privileges,
   cling only to his promise to love you.
Whether things are going well,
   or everything is falling apart,
be strong in your faithful trust,
for you will not be overcome.

May, 2010

Quoting Ps 91, Matt 7:14, Luke 9:23, John 15:18, Julian of Norwich, Showings, chapter 68.

In Well and in Woe

I was led through green meadows;
stopping to rest beside still waters;
shepherded along the right path.
It was well with my soul.

But suddenly the path I followed
led through a valley dark with death,
still waters gone, they rushed tumultuous past,
crashing, roaring over rocks,
threatening to block my way:
they overwhelmed my soul in woe.

I knew there was no turning back
to that other green and pleasant land:
there is only one way—forward.
But through my woeful hesitation
I sense the presence of others walking
this valley too—putting their arms

around me—let us go on together.
And dimly now, I sense
the presence of one like a shepherd,
up ahead of us,
leading us on with rod and staff;
well and woe mingling together in my soul.

May, 2010

Lifted and Carried

Falling, falling
into a bottomless pit,
black, cloying grief tugging at me,
disbelief weighing me down,
sinking, numb and empty—
How can I bear it?!

But I do:
a new day dawns,
life again,
and the strength to walk on—
I see, as in a dream,
that, as I am sinking,
a bubble, strong and buoyant,
forms, and lifts me up,
then another and another.
More and more emerge,
surrounding me;
lifting me,
till I see the rim of the pit;

lifting me,
till I step out onto a sunlit path.
Whenever darkness threatens,
I am lifted up.

Each bubble is a prayer,
a prayer said for me—
by friends—the nearest and the furthest:
faithful friends
carrying me
in my hour of need.

July 2010

Seeing Heaven Open

You have left us and gone on,
But gone on to where?
To heaven where you join the saints
gathered around God's throne
singing praises without end?
Have you walked from room to room
in the house of many mansions,
and found your forebears, old friends
and those you always wanted to meet?

Is it better than here—
even though here was good to you?
Is it tinged with sadness
by the absence and grieving
of those you left behind
or have you forgotten them in your rejoicing?

Where have you gone?
Gone to some place
where we will meet you again?
Or have you gone to some huge Waiting Room,
with a multitude of others,
milling around,
impatient with inactivity,
thinking that if this is heaven you want out?

Where have you gone?
Into nothingness?
A black hole?
Is this all there is in the afterwards—
Oblivion?
Is heaven just a big con?
Stephen, killed for his faith;
as he died, he saw heaven open,
God in his glory and Jesus at his side:
John, exiled for his faith;
he too saw heaven open:
Did you see it as you left?
Left with no return, unlike
Paul— lifted into the third heaven
who returned to tell of it.

Where have you gone?
Did Jesus meet you?
What are you doing?
Is it really heaven there?
One day, one day,
we will know:
For one day we will join you;
Look out for us.

January 2011

To Steve and his Spirit

He had the spirit which says,
"I can do it!
I can try, I can learn,
I can persevere,
I can do it."
        And he did.

"I can write music,
I can express my feelings in song,
I can write worship songs,
or fun songs,
or songs of protest."
        And he did.

"I can speak up when I think things are wrong,
I can speak out against hypocrisy,
I am not afraid to stand up to authority,
I can go out and protest."
        And he did.

"I can dream dreams,
I can see visions,
and go out and make them a reality.
Even if I mess up,
I can pick myself up and start again."
        And he did.

In work and play,
In his friendships,
with his family;
in all he did,
he gave his all—

throwing his heart,
his energy, his effort into it.

"I can do it,
I can do it all,
work harder,
celebrate more heartily,
eat and drink to the full,
drive faster,
cycle further,
hike longer."
        And he did.

"I can do it.
I can tube down this swollen river. . ."

21 February 2011, the first anniversary of Steve's death

Prayer on the First Anniversary of Steve's Death

God of power and energy,
Creator of all that is:
God of love and compassion,
giving your creation freedom:
God of vulnerability and weakness,
taking on our flesh and
emptying yourself for us:
God of mystery,
victor over evil and death,
yet leaving us assailed by these
on every side:

Help us to walk with you
when all is well, and we feel strong
and full of vigor,
and our love for others overflows;
Help us to keep on walking with you
when we can't understand—
when evil seems to triumph
and grief overwhelms.
May we know you are walking with us
especially in those times
when we are weak
and feel we can't go on.

Be our Mother,
hugging us and whispering
words of love and encouragement to us,
patching the hurt places,
and gently pushing us off
in the right direction again.

21 February 2011

Out of Death Comes Life

Clear and sharp
as the bright blue day around me,
the words sounded in my ear,
"Out of death comes life."
"Oh No, No!" my whole being responded—

Death is the enemy:
Death destroys all—
all we have built up,
all we hold dear,
all we look forward to,
all terminated by death.

But look at the fig tree;
twisted bare branches
reaching out, pale as ash,
a few lifeless brown leaves
desperately hanging on, trying
to pretend the tree is not dead.
Out of that dead tree,
at the right time,
shoots will appear
indistinguishable at first,
but breaking open most surely
into life.

Look at the lilies in the field:
nothing to see.
A round brown bulb
lies dead and buried,
covered with solid earth,
month after cold month,
till, at the right time
through the hard crust of soil
a green shoot thrusts
and grows and buds
into a glorious scented lily.

Death is not the enemy,
not the destroyer,
because out of death comes life.

In the darkness of death,
in the loneliness of death,
in the futurelessness of death,
can I look at the fig tree,
can I look at a flower bulb,
and believe that?

September 2011

I am the Ghost of Christmas Past

"I am the Ghost of Christmas Past;
I will stand at your side,
here in Christmas Present ,
and I will whisper, 'Remember—
remember how it was—
the family was all together then,
all full of life and vigor:
alive to the spirit of Christmas Present,
then—but Christmas Present now?'
I am the Ghost of Christmas Past;
and I will keep on whispering, 'Remember.'"

I will hear the voice of the Ghost of Christmas Past;
I will remember—its joy and its sorrow,
but I cannot live there.
So I will turn to him and say,
"Be gone now.
I have heard you,
I want to embrace Christmas Present,—
I want to be fully part of it:

it will bring its own joy,
it may even bring more joy
than you, the Ghost of Christmas Past
can bring to mind."

"I am the Ghost of Christmas Past;
And I will keep on whispering," he said.

"And I will ignore you." I replied,
as I turned my face away—
towards the present.

December 2011, Vermaaklikheid

The Curtain between two Worlds

Sometimes the curtain between two worlds is so thin
that I can see you clearly, hear you,
feel you are about to step out,
coffee cup in hand, check scarf around your neck,
cocky greeting on your lips:
the last two years of no account:
sometimes, sometimes—but fleetingly.

Mostly the curtain between two worlds is dense
as black velvet, impenetrable as a firewall,
silent as a telephone that will not ring
with an expected call.
Mostly we, on our side, are moving on,

aging, changing, going forward:
stopping often to gaze at the curtain,
realizing in reluctant sadness that
we are leaving you behind,
you, who are un-aging, unchanging,
caught forever in a snapshot moment.

We need your presence, your insight,
your cheer, but it is muffled now, and fading.
We must walk on, we cannot stop.
We must leave you behind,
till one day, one day it will be us
who push the curtain aside
to step into that other world.

20 February 2012

*Inspired by words of a poem by D. Gwenallt Jones,
from In Sensuous Glory; the poetic vision of D. Gwenallt Jones.*

From the poem, On All Soul's Eve, "The curtain between two worlds will be so thin"

When I Think Olive

One of the ideas that Steve was working on shortly before his death was a concept he named "Olive Theology." He spelled out his preliminary thoughts in an article in which he uses the olive as a metaphor for ten issues that we need to work at today. I have tried to express some of his ideas, and mine that arise from his, in a poem.

When I think olive, I think color,
the green of leaves mixed with the brown of earth,
not a lush green, not a rich earth,
but dulled down, dusty, khaki,
color of South Africa, color of Africa,
color of the Middle East.
When I think green I think green issues;
save the environment, save the rhino,
save the forests, save the wetlands:
when I think brown, I think brown issues;
dryness, drought,
lack of water, lack of food,
struggle for survival, save the people.
Which comes first, which takes precedence?
When I think olive, I think brown and green together-
integrate, adapt, survive and thrive.

When I think olive I think fruit,
oily, bitter, black or greenish,
not to be picked and eaten from the tree,
like some round red juicy apple,
but shaken, gathered, processed,
watched over, worked over, waited over,
to produce small, salty mouthfuls,
more pip than flesh,
but satisfying, even desired, food.
I think life is like that,
easy pickings mean very little;
what counts comes from watching, working, waiting.

When I think olive I think oil,
pressed in family presses, in community mills,
yellow gold, tasty and rich;
but more than that, health giving,

not oil that hardens arteries, clogs veins,
deposits fat,
but fruit and oil maintaining health.

When I think olive I think tree,
I think row upon row of trees,
stretching up and over hills, rocky and dry,
narrow leaves, fluttering, now silver, now green,
in the breeze, casting dappled shadows.
Trees mean life—more oxygen,
more soil retention,
more shelter for other creatures,
and trees point to the sacred in life,
in every culture, people, time:
their majesty, their size,
their longevity, their beauty;
all take us beyond ourselves to the Creator.

When I think olive I think age upon age,
the olive trees in Gethsemane,
the same Jesus prayed under,
twisted, gnarled trunks, porous, and cracked,
dead to our eyes, but able to re-sprout, to resurrect:
trees that talk of survival over drought, storm, time,
providing food for each generation
that comes and goes,
lives and dies,
wages war, works for peace.

When I think olive, I think olive branch,
I think peace, and I almost despair.
Who comes today carrying the olive branch?
Rather they come ripping out the trees,
destroying the ancient groves,

tearing communities apart,
destroying livelihoods, destroying people,
in Palestine, in Africa, in societies,
in families—in ourselves,
unless we think olive branch,
think peace, wage peace.

When I think olive, and I think the Bible,
Noah, his dove, and his olive branch,
the oil running down Aaron's beard,
the oil of anointing, The Chosen One, king or priest,
The Anointed One, the Messiah:
the olive tree, used by God as a symbol of peace,
of well-being for body, soul and spirit,
of Shalom, of salaam,
made one in Christ, The Anointed One,
truly human, truly God,
to make us fully human and God-like.

When I think Olive I think Steve,
his life, his work, his death,
his gifts, his legacy, his Olive Theology.
I think Steve,
and I almost despair—
but the olive points to life,
to survival, to the next generation,
to the next ones chosen
to bear the olive branch, to do theology—
to do Olive Theology.

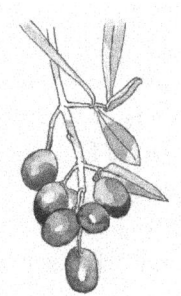

April 2012

The Chasm between Life and Death

The chasm between life and death is vast;
the traffic strictly one-way
across the huge, unbridgeable space.

But the way from life to death?
One tiny move,
one fraction of a second,
one blink of the eye,
before this word is written,
before this word is even read,
and one, fully alive, can step
across the chasm,
and be no more.

One false move,
one wrong turn,
one unseeing moment,
one careless action—
before we are even aware of it,
death swoops
and carries off its prey—
across the vast chasm.

And the empty space left
in the life of the living
can be just as vast.

February 2013

Heaven is Here Too

Evil grabs us by the throat
and says triumphantly,
"Look at me! Look at me!
Look at what I can do!
See my power—how I can
make my minions act in any
obscure little town
and the whole world
will take notice—is affected—
cowers before my power!"

But goodness is also here,
grabs us not at all,
acts unseen, unnoticed,
is disregarded, while we
attend to evil, give it
our full attention, and shrink
before its power.
There are no headlines saying,
"A group of unarmed men and women
performed an unwarranted
act of kindness."

Goodness is here, kindness is here,
love is here.
May its power grab us by the heart,
change us and spread,
flowing more freely into our world,
bringing heaven in its wake.

October, 2013

Bibliography

Allchin, Donald, D. Densil Morgan and Patrick Thomas, eds. *Sensuous Glory: The Poetic Vision of D. Gwenallt Jones.* Norwich, UK: Canterbury, 2000

Colledge, Edmond OSA and James Walsh, SJ, translators, *Julian of Norwich, Showings.* New York: Paulist, 1978

de Gruchy, Isobel. *Making All Things New: Finding Spiritual Strength with Julian of Norwich.* Norwich, UK: Canterbury, 2013, and New York: Paulist, 2013.

de Gruchy, John W, *Led into Mystery: Faith Seeking Answers in Life and Death*, London SCM Press, 2013.

Everett, William J. and John W de Gruchy, *Sawdust and Soul: A Conversation about Woodwork and Spiriuality.* Eugene. OR: Cascade, 2015.

Levy-Achtemeier, Sandra M. *Flourishing Life: Now and in the Time to Come.* Eugene, OR: Cascade, 2012.

Mankin Maria, and Maren Tirabassi, eds. *From the Psalms to the Cloud: Connecting to the Digital Age,* Cleveland: Pilgrim, 2011.

Tirabassi Maren, and Kathy Wonson Eddy, eds, *Gifts in Open Hands: More Worship Resources for the Global Community.* Cleveland: Pilgrim,2011.

The Scripture quotes are from the New Revised Standard Version Bible, copyright 1989, Division of Christian Education of the National Council of Churches of the United States of America.

The following poems were previously published in:

Gifts with Open Hands: My Prayer as a Person with Parkinson's Disease, I Pray Shalom for You, No-one Knows my Name, In Remembrance of Her, Jacob Wrestles with God.

From the Psalms to the Cloud: Sonnet to Silence.

Led into Mystery: All Shall be Well After Death?, Seeing Heaven Open.

Making All Things Well: Living in Between, All Shall be Well after Death?, You will not be Overcome.

Sawdust and Soul: When I Think Olive.

www.ingramcontent.com/pod-product-compliance
Lightning Source LLC
Chambersburg PA
CBHW071441160426
43195CB00013B/1985